LOST CITIES

Also by Valencia Robin

Ridiculous Light

LOST CITIES
POEMS
VALENCIA ROBIN

A Karen & Michael Braziller Book
PERSEA BOOKS / NEW YORK

For my mother

Copyright © 2025 by Valencia Robin

All rights reserved. No part of this publication may be reproduced or transmitted in any form or by any means, electronic or mechanical, including photocopy, audio recording, or any information storage and retrieval system, without prior permission in writing from the publisher. Request for permission or for information should be addressed to the publisher:

PERSEA BOOKS, INC.
90 Broad Street
New York, New York 10004

LIBRARY OF CONGRESS CATALOGING-IN-PUBLICATION DATA

Names: Robin, Valencia, 1958– author.
Title: Lost cities : poems / Valencia Robin.
Description: First. | New York : Persea Books, 2025. | "A Karen & Michael Braziller Book." | Summary: "Brimming with music, bursting with flora, the poems in Valencia Robin's second collection are both a walking tour of local neighborhoods and a journey into space and across time, ways of looking and listening to the past in order to find our best way forward. Engaging with artistic heroes like James Baldwin, Amiri Baraka, Gwendolyn Brooks, Etheridge Knight, Audre Lorde, Nina Simone, Pablo Neruda, and Stevie Wonder, Valencia Robin looks for guidance, grounding, and even hope in spite of the traumas she witnesses and experiences daily"—Provided by publisher.
Identifiers: LCCN 2025002405 (print) | LCCN 2025002406 (ebook) |
    ISBN 9780892556151 (paperback) | ISBN 9780892556168 (ebook)
Subjects: LCGFT: Poetry.
Classification: LCC PS3618.O317594 L63 2025 (print) | LCC PS3618.O317594 (ebook) |
    DDC 811/.6—dc23/eng/20250127
LC record available at https://lccn.loc.gov/2025002405
LC ebook record available at https://lccn.loc.gov/2025002406

Book design and composition by Rita Skingle
Typeset in Quinn
Manufactured in the United States of America.
Printed on acid-free paper.

CONTENTS

ONE

First Walk of the New Year / 3

Poetry / 4

Ask Your Grandmother / 5

Poem for the Guy Down the Street / 6

Letter to Charlottesville / 7

After Graduate School / 8

Song / 9

Sometimes life feels like daytime TV / 10

Hi / 12

New Day / 13

Mattie / 14

For instance / 15

Help / 16

At the ER / 17

The Afro / 18

Sometimes we just like someone / 19

Gone Hour / 20

Woke / 22

Atlantis / 24

TWO

Lt. Uhura, Communications Officer, Star Trek / 27

THREE

Non-essential Worker / 37

Zoom / 39

The Daily Show / 40

Driving home / 41

In the Waiting Area / 42

Confessions / 44

November After the Vaccine / 45

Abstract Painting / 46

Late / 47

The Residency / 49

In the future / 51

Ars Poetica / 52

Notes / 53

Acknowledgments / 55

I lost two cities, lovely ones.
—Elizabeth Bishop

the flights of this journey
mapless   uncertain
and necessary as water
—Audre Lorde

ONE

First Walk of the New Year

Little wiener dog doing his best show horse,
jumping one, two, three stumps in a row,
his boy is too busy scrolling to notice, but I smile
all the way up the hill. Bitter cold
yet this curious stand of trees with green leaves
—not magnolia, not holly. A man's walking boot
tied to a NO TRESPASSING sign, a brown kestrel
high on a branch spreading her wings,
the shock of cloud-color underneath.
I think of the conversation last night, four women
in the kitchen eating popcorn and olives,
how quick I was to roll my eyes, say who has time
—as if love was a second job, as if joy could wait,
as if my heart was the kid on the phone
and not the little dog.

Poetry

after Pablo Neruda

And then everything changed,
not that anyone would notice.
I still take the stairs, still feel helpless
when I'm driving and the sun blinds me,
still imagine tackling the school shooter
after every school shooting,
gouging out their eyes with my fingers,
still praying Eros and Cupid haven't forgotten
me, still remember when T said she couldn't stop
crying, that just the light coming through
the window could crush her—still see her face
when I said she might be menopausal. Missing
the mourning doves—still mad at that hawk.
And who misses the sound of sweet potatoes boiling,
the lid clanging the night before Thanksgiving.
Still holding on to that jar of old keys for no reason—
my dead mother's keys, her dead mother's keys,
keys to every home I've ever had. And
this morning, still staring out the window
watching the wind whip up the fallen
leaves like a swarm of low flying swallows. Still
watching minutes later and minutes after that.

Ask Your Grandmother

*for Adrianne Finelli
and her grandmother, Lucille Mary Koehler*

Ask your grandmother
why she had six children,
your mother's mother
who was good at math and science,
yet got married straight out of high school,
your *nana*, your *yaya*
who, after the first two, told her doctor
that was it, but he said No, the rule was six
and after the third one when she thought she would lose her mind
and after the fifth one when she did, he said No again,
your grandmother, who was poor
but not Mexican or Native American or Black
and so never had to worry about going to the state clinic
for an appendectomy and leaving without her uterus—no,
she was white and married which meant she could have as many
    children
as her doctor, the AMA—some guys in a room—decided,
your grandmother who's looking at you as if to say,
you've been to college—how could you not know this?

Poem for the Guy Down the Street

He used to call me *Darling*.
Every morning, *How ya doin', Darlin'*.
Beefy, coffee-colored,
thirty if that,
yet something already Sisyphean
about him, forever hunched
under the hood of his taxi,
pulling out the engine
twice that one week.
Wherever he is,
may he catch a break,
in this life *and* the next,
if the world is just a hologram,
a mass daydream we're all having
may we imagine that anyone
who can take apart an engine
can afford a house with a garage and why not
make all the engines electric now,
too, decide that the engine pulling every possible lever
to keep those two things from happening
is running for its life. We could do that.
And yet—can we keep the *Darling*,
keep it and not mean anything by it? Can we
ever not love the way he said it?

Letter to Charlottesville

after August 12, 2017

I came here for poetry. Left a paycheck and friends
I won't find anywhere else, a city of trees
and long walks around a river
that was my therapist, that I wish I could call.
Funny how Virginia has always been ground zero
—Jamestown, John Brown, even the shore
where those first stolen Africans landed,
none of which I thought about as I walked to campus,
as I practically skipped to class. I saw that statue
once. It was like turning down a dark alley,
like a noose on a pedestal in the middle of a park,
and who puts something like that in a park,
Charlottesville—city my cousins will never mistake for Charlotte
again, college town that was never just a college town,
battleground long before those men were met
by your *bankers and drummers*, your sons and daughters
one of whom did not come home, who belongs to all of us
now. And is this where we live, Charlottesville?
College town, battleground, city that gave me
my first mountains—and what about these hills
that plunge and climb like amusement park rides,
foothills they call them. Hills I'll never walk the same
way again but, no, I won't be giving them back.

After Graduate School

Needless to say, I support the forsythia's war
against the dull colored houses, the beagle
deciphering the infinitely complicated universe
at the bottom of a fence post. I should be gussying up
my resume, I should be dusting off my protestant work ethic,
not walking around the neighborhood loving the peonies
and the lilac bushes, not heading up Shamrock
and spotting Lucia coming down the train tracks. Lucia
who just sold her first story and whose rent is going up,
too, Lucia who's moving to South America to save money,
Lucia, cute twenty-something I wish wasn't walking down train tracks
alone. I tell her about my niece teaching in China, about the waiter
who built a tiny house in Hawaii, how he saved up, how
he had to call the house a garage to get a building permit.
Someone's practicing the trumpet, someone's frying bacon
and once again the wisteria across the street is trying to take over
the nation. Which could use a nice invasion, old growth trees
and sea turtles, every kind of bird marching
on Washington. If I had something in my refrigerator,
if my house didn't look like the woman who lives there
forgot to water the plants, I'd invite Lucia home,
enjoy another hour of not thinking about not having a job,
about not having a mother to move back in with.
I could pick Lucia's brain about our circadian rhythms,
about this space between sunrise and sunset,
ask if she's ever managed to get inside it, the air,
the sky ethereal as all get out—*so close*
and no ladder in sight.

Song

> *Where were you when I needed you last winter?*
> —Stevie Wonder, "Superwoman"

O sound organized in time, O simple question
bluing up the ordinary, merging with the rain
outside, that grimy fan in the corner. No one
my age should willingly come to this lost city,
hear this man sing *I need you, baby* and hit replay.
O worms waiting patiently, O funny hope lifting me up
for as long as I can remember, planning my escape
—you win, let's climb off this high horse, be a body.
No, don't call it nostalgia, not when I'm trying so hard
not to wake the neighbors. Call it elegy, fathers missing
in action, a husband I should've dragged to therapy,
that once there was a boy who said if I *didn't*, it was over
—probably you've met him—that as I stood behind him
in the foyer crying, begging the way only first love can,
I caught his grin in the mirror. And how to put *that* to music,
hover above the melody so you can see how completely I owned him
afterwards, how cruel a sixteen-year-old girl can be. I talk
about it to myself all the time, love and the moment after,
longing carrying us to some other country, a place
we pretend we've never been, not quite sure
we're pretending. Lover, I have not seen
or heard from, asking me where I was last winter,
as if I haven't been right here waiting
—all my life, Mr. Wonder. All my life.

Sometimes life feels like daytime TV,

like a game show or some other excuse
for selling toothpaste. Wish I could remember who said that,
some writer describing how it feels when she can't write,
nailing it, not that I'm not guilty of a certain mindlessness,
not that I don't like the convenience of toothpaste,
of salmon already filleted in a vacuum-packed pouch,
of disposable razors and individually packaged strawberry yogurt
—of throwing it all away whenever I feel like it. And to think—*just
   that*,
the mountains and mountains of trash—in the ocean, dumped
where we can't see it—Black and brown people living around it
like company towns, working it like a nine to five.
And what would it take for me to try the co-op's bulk toothpaste,
to remember to bring my reusable bags,
to *own* it—the deluge of bottles and baby dolls,
of Easter baskets and string bikinis. Or little Buddhas
like the one I found the other day while vacuuming
—tiny burgundy Buddha I have no memory of buying
or being given, wondering where it came from
before noticing my neighbor out the window
curiously hoisting his dog into the air, the twenty-something
who'd offered his shovel when my piece of crap broke,
the dog not small, some kind of retriever mix,
yet my neighbor was lifting her like a father
lifts his child to see the moon or the Milky Way,
holding her there for a good twenty seconds
before folding the animal into his arms

and cradling her like a baby,
the dog looking around as if embarrassed,
but the guy just standing there
and me watching, still
thumbing that piece of plastic.

Hi

There's a brother who sits over on North University.
Looks like James Baldwin in a doo-rag. Sings.
Is he homeless? People give him money
like he's homeless. I look the other way,
cross the street if I see him in time,
although one day I don't see him in time
and without meaning to I look into his eyes.
He says *Hi*. So, what can I do? I say *Hi*.
Which means the next time I see him I have to
say *Hi*. And the next time, *Hi. Hi.* And
the next time, too. That's the seminal text
of our conversation, the full operatic range
of whatever we are to each other. He says *Hi*,
I say *Hi*. I say *Hi*, he says *Hi—Hi, Hi,
Hi, Hi*. No idea of what the other
might say next.

New Day

If we perceive barely a sliver of our reality,
what's knowable only a small part of what's out there,

that fat bee bumping up against the window,
the faint sound of a neighbor's car radio.

And if neither here nor there is where we are
then perhaps the Sunrise Nursing Home is the dawn,

is the new day, perhaps leaving your mother with a stranger
not unlike her—divorced with three kids, threatened

with dismissal if she refuses to work a double shift—
perhaps this is the white flag the world has been waiting for,

the moment before the universe says, *Just kidding*
and you can turn around and drive your mother back

to a house that's wheelchair accessible, to the English teacher
you hoped was in your future

or perhaps a sister who likes being in charge, loves
to be right, so that every decision you don't want to make,

so that whatever reality is or isn't,
at least you're not in there by yourself.

Mattie

Today the river is a dark clock.
I walk the narrow path around it,
my way edged with spent poppies
my mind a little lost,
searching for those days
of too many cousins to count, you
and your sisters, four beauties
in a family known for its Helens
if thankfully not its Troys. And
you were so funny, well past eighty
and still able to drive us to the family cemetery,
to climb on top of Uncle Henry's head stone
and point to our dead, to call each name
while eating a handful of grapes.
And now it's your name that's been called,
your stories we're telling, the days passing
so quickly, I can almost feel the world turning.

For instance,

take the insomniac staring into Monday
morning, would-be instrument of music
wishing she had the day off, searching
the sketches of light and shadow on the wall
for a sign—little girl who did not get away,
woman about to be late. She thought
about the father she'd never met,
the death bed confession her therapist said
most men took to their graves.
She thought about his son,
the brother she didn't know existed,
calling her not long after the funeral,
no idea he was calling on her birthday.
And what of other such surprise parties,
eerie timing refusing to add up—moments
so unlike the day she was dreading,
not that everyday could be strange,
the world not what it seems,
yet how long since something had taken her
between its thumb and forefinger,
shined her up like a lucky penny?

Help

> *Oh, how I long to know the truth*
> —Nina Simone

So many *distractions*. Today the popular tourist spot
I always have to warn my out-of-town guests about,
the famous house they always want to see anyway,
have to see perhaps, have to hear, listen
to the story of its celebrated owner,
all the careful details of his life in that legendary house
and marvel, truly marvel (although why so surprised?)
at how rarely we'll hear the words plantation
or enslaved person. I watch the class of high schoolers
ahead of us, their sullen, resentful Black faces
reminding me of my sullen, resentful Black face
forty years earlier, resisting with no idea I was
part of the resistance, no clue that rolling my eyes
was saving me, that there are all kinds of lifeboats
—long walks after school, the art I spent hours
making that I never called art or if I was lucky,
a book or CD from the public library (Nina,
Audre Lorde, Greg Tate), the mother lodes
I just happened to stumble on—the teachers
I never found at school, the ones who took me to church,
put me to work.

At the ER

He'd given me a local by then,
was stitching my numbed palm
back together, holding my hand
open and steady, me watching,
waiting for him to look at me
though I had no sense that I was
waiting for him to look at me,
that soon we'd be smiling,
smiling. And was it the first smile
two people ever smiled, the oldest
smile in the world? Then the ride home
with my husband, the roar in my ears
slowly dissipating as I said yes
to pizza. And for years, this habit
of pressing my thumb into my palm
and circling the small, hard scar
that nobody can see except for me.

The Afro

Walking in the last of the light,
the last of autumn, the leaves blistered
and fevered, a shimmy of sunset and traffic, people
trying to get home. I think of my color-blind friend
before her corrective glasses—no green, no red tips
of maples purpled by the sky. I think of my own sight
correction—my mind, my hair on the same page
for the first time, bringing them both to work,
first job out of college, all-white department,
my colleagues looking affronted, the VP calling
me to his office—me, the rebel with the chintz sofa,
me, the radical hooked on space movies and spy novels,
—yes, me and all my unexamined ways of being,
all my sources of confusion sitting there listening
as my silent masses burned and looted.
One of my colleagues apologized. I started writing
a novel and for a minute everything in the world
that made me, was so clear.

Sometimes we just like someone,

no reason, just something about them,
sometimes the river we're passing with barely a glance
pulls us to its edge and stands us there,
sky-hypnotized, sun-varnished. This morning
it walks me back to my girlhood, back
to how I held myself in, held myself in, afraid
of being too happy in my sister's territory,
back to my cousin Terry, his black curls,
his still water my nation, my city
of brotherly love. Gwendolyn Brooks once asked,
And if sun comes, how shall we greet him?
to which Etheridge Knight replied
from the Indiana State Prison,
The sun came, Miss Brooks.
And oh, the smile, the plume, the kin
in her voice when she introduced him
and his poem, said *Etheridge,*
come here and open your mouth.
Did I mention that I stopped
sucking my thumb
before my cousin Terry,
that I went cold turkey
because he was a year older,
because he'd *always* be a year older.
His big brothers teased him relentlessly,
yet he's never once taken his revenge.

Gone Hour

Within minutes
we cover the strange weather,
the race work, the gender work,
all the heavy lifting
not in our job descriptions.
Then T remembers the photos
from her niece's wedding, the preemie
who wasn't supposed to live,
puts familiar names with faces,
catches me up on knee replacements
and third marriages, retirements
and part-time jobs to keep busy, talking
over the cacophony of espresso machines
and Sunday brunch conversations
reminiscent of how many tofu scrambles
with extra crispy rosemary potatoes,
how many absent-minded waiters
yet to bring my silverware? I hug Ngozi
on my way back from getting a fork
and when she points to her son
—our server—nothing can save me,
every gone hour, every disappeared year
refusing to be just seconds ago. Back at the table,
something T says about her sister
with cancer reminds me of my mother,
the tenderness I couldn't give her
that I paid for when I tried. My tea is cold,
still, I thank Amiri for the slices of lemon,

manage not to tell him I once changed his diaper.
T takes my picture and please explain why
as soon as she sat down my whole world
calibrated. Outside, the budding trees
are coloring yet another grey day baby green.
Ngozi arrives with hot, licorice tea,
scoots in like old times.

Woke

No voices or angels, no psychedelics
or kundalini awakening, no dying

and coming back a different person,
sounding cuckoo

and looking for a book deal
—yes, meeting your Maker

yet still needing to buy groceries.
Nothing like that.

You're simply walking from your office
to Monday morning staff meeting,

heading down a long corridor,
white walls as far as the eye can see,

a day that's the opposite of supernatural,
a morning that couldn't be less mystical,

when—and how else to say it—the universe blinks
and everything there is to know yawns into you

and you into it. Everything. Not like a book with pages
you have to turn or thoughts you have to think,

but as simultaneous and endless as space.
How long does it last? Seconds

before you're back in the world, back in your life
—first professional in the family, hating every minute,

first black person in the office, ready to kill somebody.
And all your new found brilliance? Gone

like a flock of geese taking off, like a song
from a passing car, like a dream

that won't come back
yet lives on the tip of your tongue.

Atlantis

after Eavan Boland

Where could it be, I often wonder.
Empire, island, house on Spring Street
—me and Claude, T in the spare room—
how could it all disappear,
yet feel as if it's just around the corner?
Our movie nights and favorite-poem parties,
our lazy Sundays with Coltrane and Edith Piaf,
Claude's crepes back before anyone had heard of Nutella.
Then I found his secret drawer, that treasure chest
of letters and post cards and so much for Shangri-la.
And when T said she couldn't take another Michigan winter
I proofread her CV, strangely clueless that I was helping her
leave. And were those days the closest I'll ever get to it,
each new sighting just a reminder of what we've lost
—no, not some grand legend, Plato getting allegorical,
better that old song by the Isley Brothers—remember?
That swelling voice, that withering guitar shipwrecking us.

TWO

Lt. Uhura, Communications Officer, Star Trek

[Episode 1: Beyond the Beyond]

No one ever talked in my family,
is that why I chose communications,
all that silence, the sound
of my brilliant, overworked parents
ignoring their children? And why
the Enterprise? How many times can I say
Hailing frequencies open, Captain
and listen for something bigger than me?
How many ways can I translate
this emptiness, this distance between things?
And could this uniform be any tighter?
Not that I'd rather be selling real estate
on the moon or teaching the next generation
the same grand narratives I was taught. No,
it's not the job and yet, after years of talking
for a living, this sudden urge to say something.
And it came on like fever, a desire
like a name on the tip of my tongue
and is it *my* name, *my* strange new worlds
waiting to be discovered? I watch the Captain
climb into his big chair, smile out into God
knows what, calmly say what he said
the week before: *Space, the final frontier—*
as if the stars, the moons aren't right here
in us, as if saving the day and the next day
and the next will ever fill him up,

as if what I'm after isn't its own fool's errand.
Although, that was last week's episode. Today,
the hair on the back of my neck stands up
and the heart points.

[EPISODE 2: INSIDE WOMAN]

Don't let the spaceship fool you,
it's cowboys and Indians up here.
Show me an alien species
who's not interested in turning the cosmos
into condos and I'll show you this season's
bad guy, show me an indigenous being
who's hell-bent on stopping its planet
from being strip-mined and—well,
you get the idea. None of which I thought
about before joining the Enterprise.
I just wanted to be the first
Black woman to see the universe
who wasn't cooking and cleaning,
wanted to bask in all the fan mail
the network refused to give me.
I would've gone back to Broadway
if Dr. King hadn't begged me to stay,
said thanks to me Black children
and white children, *Jews and gentiles,
protestants and Catholics*
wanted to be astronauts
or to play one on TV,
insisted I had a bigger role to play
this look in his eyes,
like he'd live to see it.

[Episode 3: First Kiss, 1968]

Who wasn't holding their breath
after Kirk and I locked lips? And yet no death
threats, no Klan marches, no cancellation.
In fact, turn on the TV today and you'd think
that kiss had fixed everything—couples
of every combination, a kaleidoscope
of happy people and every one of them
trying to sell us something. Almost
as if humanity has turned a corner, almost
as if Marketing has done some research,
almost as if
  George

Breonna

       Ahmaud
  Sandra

 Tamir
Michael

   and Trayvon

lived in some galaxy far, far away.

[EPISODE 4: MIND MELD ME]

Boldly going where no Black woman has gone before
can get old—the pay equity
Spock had to force the network to give me,
the fear that my afro would scare viewers
away, winning that fight only to have my lines cut
because Kirk thought he was the only star
in the galaxy. Spock was like a *brother
from another planet* through it all, I lived
for that raised eyebrow, his icy cool
whenever *Mr. Captain* sucked all the air
out of the room, those pointy ears
like red meat to the Dr. McCoys of the world
and is that why Sulu and I got treated like humans?
The writers made us lovers in the reboots,
forgot that Vulcans don't get jiggy very often,
not that what we had wasn't libidinal in some sense.
Because how great is it to love what you do, the thrill
when the energy—ours and the rest of the crew's,
took on a life of its own, became a single thought
because the Klingons or Romulans
were about to blow us to smithereens,
—yes, despite the same old script,
(battles, battles and more battles)
whenever we were together
a different story always seemed possible.

[EPISODE 5: MORE]

There was this episode once,
our mission to reach the unreachable
as usual, nothing but static
in my ear and yet something had us
and wouldn't let go. Again and again
I asked it to identify itself, clearly
it wanted something or were we
anthropomorphizing again,
our human sense the only sense,
always some boogie man?
And in the book of life
does it always come back to this?
Telling stories so we can sleep at night,
convince ourselves this isn't a one-way trip.
And surprise, surprise—all this intelligent life
but still, no one who really gets us.
Of course, sixty minutes isn't a lot of time
—fifty if you count the commercials.
After shaking us up, whatever it was
turned out *not* to be all powerful after all.
Was it lonely? Curious? Perhaps
we're all just turning our little knobs
and waving our tiny antenna,
asking for it
and when the unknown

answers, we scream
like children, *Again, again!*

THREE

Non-essential Worker

Computer gone dark, sun going down,
too late to go walking so walk the room,

the house. Travel the walls, the books, the philodendron
with its tender new leaves, old friend and now coworker

doing wonders for that corner. Leave behind the work day,
the hard labor of doing little that requires imagination,

that pays the rent and won't put you on a ventilator. Recall
this morning's red balloon of possibility—the promise to meditate,

to start that film script, to not recognize yourself
by the end of the day. Don't open that bag of popcorn.

OK, fine, but don't eat the whole thing. Notice
how quickly your empty house has become an empty house

again. How about some music, no words, just strings, a melody
like mist rising from a green pond. Try to be green, too—

yellow-green, blue-green, plant yourself
in that long reaching, yearn like a woman

trying to build something holy in her spare time.
Forget about a better job, how much salt

is in that popcorn, be a wave, be a particle,
turn to see the night staring in like a giant pupil.

What are you anyway? Dust, light, tiny speck
doing bad pirouettes around the room,

touching your toes, talking to the philodendron,
anything not to think about the news.

Zoom

> *I'd like to fly away*
> —The Commodores, "Zoom"

Has a name ever broken more promises?
Virtual staff meetings? Remote learning?
Lionel Ritchie and the Commodores should sue,
if not for themselves, for all the unsuspecting bodies
instantly transported back to the Buffet Room,
back to that furnace of wall-to-wall people
coupling up, not one of us thinking
about killer viruses or crushing loneliness,
the night a well-oiled machine,
my head a wet mop,
my feet, my feet, my feet.
Yet who could say no to flying—*zooming*,
forgetting if only for a few minutes
that I was failing Math 101. Despite the title,
the tune taking its time, rocking us slowly,
inexorably beyond caring who we were rocking
with—arms, legs, sweat—our bodies
filling the room with plumes of rocket fuel,
our gorgeous, combustible bodies
humming, swaying, touching, craving,
delighting, savoring—the kind of technology
that takes millions of years to perfect.

The Daily Show

The cream-colored walls
I never notice
unless there's a spider
in the corner, this box
I've spent one day too many in
—the books and more books,
the reminders on the mirror,
even the sunny window
has broken its promises,
the backyard's junky jumble
of poplars and maples, the limbs
and kudzu reaching up to form
a large, black hole that I'm refusing
to call a portal, though as soon as I notice
it, a cardinal darts in and disappears.
And all morning the sound of the boy
next door hitting baseballs,
the sharp crack each time the ball
meets the bat, nonstop
thanks to the new pitching machine
no one asked me about. And now
the sound of his little brother
wanting next,
three more hits before I hear
Ok, followed by, *Wait—like this.*
No, not the least bit annoyed,
killing me with his patience.

Driving home,

nothing spectacular happening,

no epiphany, no booming voice saying, *Behold*
like back in Sunday school. Still, somehow, I'm free

of the heartache I keep folded in my back pocket—the news
I've stopped watching, the rage that won't stop following me,

the fantasies straight out of Greek mythology, only it's me
—my horse, my chariot dragging Hector's dead body.

And what is it that lifts me out of that inferno,
sets me down inside this respite, this startling stillness,

although that sounds too pretty, too self-important—it's more
like that overgrown lot I'm passing, totally random

and filled with something purple.

In the Waiting Area

The first vaccine was in an old JC Penney,
the National Guard running things.
When it was my turn, I lifted my sleeve
and *loved* every second of that needle going in.
I was still in Charlottesville where I'd come to study poetry—
a last mad midlife Hail Mary to sing my song—
and where I'd found a job—*Oh marvelous timing*—
just months before the shutdown. Maybe a dozen others
were already waiting their fifteen minutes, all staring
at their phones, all except an elderly Black woman on oxygen
and a man who was probably her son. Otherwise, no eye contact,
no thumbs up, no woo-hoo we made it, yet as soon as I sat down, a peace
I didn't know I was missing settled over me like a shawl. I smiled
at the old woman from behind my mask, thought about my mother
on oxygen her last months. The rain on the roof slowed then stopped.
I smiled at the old woman again, wondered if she was smiling back.
My mind drifted to the story about switched babies in Newfoundland,
two men in their fifties, new coworkers with the same birthday
and a scary resemblance to each other's family, the story
of an overcrowded maternity clinic and dozens of remote fishing villages,
the story of a head nurse that everyone blamed, the story of Newfoundland
all the way back to the first Europeans and the Beothuk who they wiped out.
I'd read the whole thing, the two men suing—reeling,
no idea who they were now, their siblings hit by a truck, too,

several elderly women coming forward with their *almost* switched baby
stories—reliving the terror. No more mention of the Beothuk,
though I could feel them wanting to say something. And yet,
that strange calm, if that's even the right word, as if my body
and the bodies around me were somehow celebrating without us.
Did that head nurse switch those babies on purpose?
Was this really my life? All alone in this town—no family, no tribe
—work, yes, I could do from home, sad factory of email
and Zoom meetings, long walks around the neighborhood afterwards
—the raucous birds, the lush yards—the dull longing for the lives inside
the houses I was passing, forgetting I'd had a house, had a husband (two),
that before poetry, I'd been even lonelier. The old woman on oxygen
and her son stood up to leave, which meant it was almost my time,
too. She gave me a thumbs up as she walked by. I'm still waving.

Confessions

I confess when I watch the big award shows on TV
I still think that could be me up there thanking people,
my mother, my grandmother, my entire collective
in the hereafter screaming, beaming down to join me,
my father wondering if he can come, too.
I admit to everything including wanting to kidnap
the young dread knocked out in front of the Paramount
and not setting him free until he's marriage material. I know
I should want to send him back to his community
to start a farmers' market or space program, to help us
expand into previously unknown aspects of being.
But first I want him to take my little neighbor to a play.
I'm the person who sees the happy baby and aches
to climb into the mother's lap, who routinely falls for trees,
their wide, open arms beckoning. My painting helps,
though most days it's just my dream of painting. Last night
this woman kept referring to her father as daddy
—*daddy this, daddy that*—as if he was everybody's daddy.
My current form of self-medication are the hours between 6 and 8 AM,
the day slowly dressing itself, the light touching me. Sometimes
I watch the news, sometimes I love all that hate. Then there's beauty
(with the little b) that heartless time suck. Still—all my life
I've been screaming *Daddy, daddy!* and so many people
—friends, strangers—have come running.

November After the Vaccine

in memory of Patricia Jackson Ward

How to talk about the trees this fall, Pat,
this desire to slowly undress,
that sense of being translated
into a dozen languages
and I've only been walking
for a few minutes. You tell me
how a red can be so purple, that yellow
not just yellow but a primordial almost green,
loud, loud like you—laughing, screaming
singing, *Hot damn, call the police
and the fireman*, refusing to be shushed,
to care about the time or where we were.
Yes, a rainbow flag and—thank you—
three Black Lives Matter signs
in a neighborhood with few Black people,
with hills and gullies, a blue jay married
to a small, lemon gingko. Other walkers
smile and wave as if it's all been a bad dream,
as if we aren't still giving each other six feet. And
that thicket of hickories crowned not orange but peach?
Show offs. Minor gods. The sky, the clouds feeling themselves,
too. As if California isn't on fire, as if Black lives really do matter.
Even the sour apple candy I find in my pocket, even the red fox
in the driveway of matching leaves, the pink mask hanging
on a fence. I pull out my phone to catch an old oak in all its bliss
or is that you getting the party started again?

Abstract Painting

Her nephew, the tax attorney,
her nephew her heart
asks what the painting she's painting
means, assumes she knows the answer,
that there *is* an answer
beyond the urge to make something,
the feeling she wakes to every morning
and, oh, the blanket of starlings
covering the lawn of this house
she never thought she'd own, only trying
because the guy she was dating
said she'd never get a mortgage. And
if only she could've harnessed that mettle,
she'd use it now for what really matters—
a better jerk detector, more time with her nephew
or a painting that means whatever
dozens of iridescent black bodies mean
when they take off and land, take off and land.

Late

Do movie memories even count? And why
this one? Judd Hirsch, a detective driving
down the highway with his young son
on his day off, the two of them singing
"Oh, What a Beautiful Morning,"
as the camera cuts to Judd noticing
the name of the same street
as the woman who won't stop calling
the mother of the missing boy,
the *crank* or so he thinks
because it's been a year and they've all been *cranks*.
In the movie, she sounds old and Black, begs the boy's mother
to come get her son, brags that she just finished having lunch
with Jesus. She's not happy when Judd shows up at her house
unannounced, barks to see his badge, her rage biblical
if not suicidal considering she's talking to a New York City cop.
But it's the movies so Judd flinches like the rest of us,
fumbles for his wallet, some part of me trying to remember
what people used to call women like her. And,
of course, the missing boy is right next door,
answers when Judd knocks, an old white woman
on a walker hurrying up behind him, complaining
they had to take him, she needed help,
her brother worked nights—and did the screenwriter
mean for us to see in her logic the same logic
that built this country? Back in Judd's car,
the missing boy—who must be old enough
to have his own kids by now—asks if he's under arrest,

and aren't we glad Judd left his engineering job
at Westinghouse to try acting, aren't we happy
he gets to stare into the rearview mirror
for a long second before saying, *No, honey*
and something else that doesn't matter
because apparently that's what I've been waiting for
—not the camera cutting to the boy's mother
turning the corner, not the boy spotting her first—no,
it's that *Honey* and those German Shepherd eyes
wishing they'd listened to that Old Battle Axe
sooner, that would give up sunsets or singing
for a chance to save the day better.
That's why I'll be late for work,
why the two-minute shower, why
I'll have to grab my make-up to put on later.

The Residency

In between moving house
and starting a new gig,
a castle in the Italian countryside
complete with a turret
and a dozen other fellows
every night at dinner.
Three weeks of waking
to a fit of chimney swifts
—their alley-oops and nose dives
inches from my window,
of cypresses tall as castles
in the distance, coniferous
rocket ships minus the countdown
and any sense of rush, rush, rush.
Three weeks of walking
the streets that Piero walked—
the famous churches, the divine views—
sipping a decaf soy cappuccino
worrying about *not* worrying
about anything. Three weeks of bonding
with twelve strangers over you-name-it,
fried zucchini blossoms filled with mash potatoes,
the ping pong and billiards we sucked at,
the writing I wasn't doing, the news I didn't watch,
the world that didn't care, coming home
jet-lagged and a little sad, a little sad,
already missing our little Alexandria
(or was it Never-Never Land?),

opening the blinds only to find
three cypress trees I'd never noticed.

In the future,

you will finally write a poem
beyond the limits of where you usually work,
one so much smarter than you,
almost as if you opened a channel
and something came through, a voice,
a guide, perhaps some famous dead poet
gifting you a poem just for the fun of it,
no, not trying to impress, death has freed them
of all that, freed them of everything
except this clumsy search for Beauty,
this weakness for bliss—maybe death
only magnifies those hungers, which is why
people reincarnate—have you seen the research
at the University of Virginia—again and again you
have apparently kissed that brilliant light goodbye,
waved away those waves of unconditional love,
not to mention your mother, the-cousins-like-mothers
and the father you will never meet in this world, yes,
left all that to come back here
to where it's so dark
you're happy for a single match,
a light switch.

Ars Poetica

I woke up singing
my favorite song as a kid
and I mean, really singing,
catching myself all morning,
asking myself what it means,
a reminder perhaps
that we can be strange
—we wake, we sing,
we wonder why we're singing,
we realize how seldom we have a song
in us anymore, remember how we
used to play/be Aretha and Anita
or Earth, Wind and Fire—Maurice
bringing it, sending us on one of the few oldies
where the words 'right on' don't sound silly,
standing in the middle of the room
giving our all to the olive-green sofa
and wood paneling, mama at work
—we even had his little laugh down
and when's the last time we believed
what we were saying so completely,
all that 70's positivity, all that gospel
pretending to be the devil's music
—and is that what ruined us, why we're so bad
at real life—practically screaming the last line,
And if there ain't no beauty, you gotta make some beauty,
deciding without even knowing we'd decided
that *that*—Lord help us—was the dream.

NOTES

"Poetry" is inspired by Pablo Neruda's poem "Poetry."

"Ask Your Grandmother" is inspired by artist and filmmaker Adrianne Finelli and her grandmother, Lucille Mary Koehler. The poem references the difficulty, historically, for American women to get a surgical procedure called tubal ligation (more commonly known as *getting one's tubes tied*) in order to prevent pregnancy.

The poem also references the United States' forced sterilization and eugenics program which varied from state to state. For instance, beginning in 1909 and continuing for 70 years, California led the country in the number of sterilization procedures performed on both men and women. In other states, forced sterilization of Native Americans persisted into the 1970s and 1980s. "Mississippi appendectomies" was another name for unnecessary hysterectomies performed at teaching hospitals in the South on women of color as practice for medical students. The famed civil rights leader, Fannie Lou Hamer, who coined the term, was one of those women.

"Letter to Charlottesville" is written in response to the largest gathering of white supremacists in a generation. The rally was held in Charlottesville, Virginia from August 11 to 12, 2017. One of the organizers' stated goals was to stop the proposed removal of the statue of Confederate General Robert E. Lee from Charlottesville's former Lee Park.

The white supremacist marchers were met by counter protesters and Charlottesville resident Heather Heyer was killed and 35 other counter protesters were injured when a self-identified white supremacist deliberately drove his car into them as they were leaving.

"Help" references Thomas Jefferson's Monticello, a 5,000-acre working plantation in Charlottesville, Virginia where over 400 enslaved men, women and children were bought, sold and forced to work.

"Sometimes we just like someone," references a recording of Gwendolyn Brooks and Etheridge Knight on February 25, 1986.

"Atlantis" is inspired by Eavan Boland's poem "Atlantis—A Lost Sonnet" as well as the R&B classic "Voyage to Atlantis" by the Isley Brothers.

"Lt. Uhura, Communications Officer, Star Trek" references Nyota Uhura or simply Uhura, a fictional character in the Star Trek franchise. In the original television series, the character was portrayed by Nichelle Nichols, who reprised the role for the first six Star Trek feature films. Uhura was one of the first black characters to be portrayed in a non-menial role on an American television series.

"Late" references the movie *Without a Trace*.

"Ars Poetica" is inspired by the song "All About Love" by Earth, Wind & Fire, which was written and sung by Maurice White, the group's founder.

ACKNOWLEDGMENTS

Thank you to the editors of the following journals, podcasts and anthologies in which some of the poems in this book have appeared or are forthcoming:

The Virginia Quarterly Review, The Boston Review, The Best American Poetry 2022, the Academy of American Poets' *Poem-a-Day, The Southern Poetry Anthology Volume IX: Virginia, Emerging Form* Podcast, *Hampden Sydney Poetry Review, Phi Kappa Phi Forum, Zócola Public Square, Poetry Unbound Podcast, High Country News, The National Poetry Review,* and *The Adroit Journal.*

I wish to thank the following institutions for their generous support: The National Endowment of the Arts, Cave Canem, East Tennessee State University and the Civitella Ranieri Artist Residency.

Thank you to Toi Derricotte, Cornelius Eady, Ruth Ellen Kocher, Dawn Lundy Martin and Willie Perdomo for their generous instruction. Thank you to the fellows and staff at Cave Canem and the Civitella Ranieri Artist Residency. Thank you to Jesse Graves for his generosity and support. And I am especially grateful to Anna, Lindsay, Aran, Erika and Irène for providing invaluable feedback on drafts of these poems.

None of this work would have been possible without the love and support of my family and friends.

Finally, thank you to everyone at Persea Books, most notably Gabe Fried.